FROM MY PERSPECTIVE...

A Guide to University and College Career Centre Management

Dedicated to the Memory of
Joy Powdhar

A University of Toronto Career Centre
Valued Colleague and Friend
(1963 – 2007)

From My Perspective...A Guide to University and College Career Centre Management

Published and distributed in 2009 by
The Canadian Education and Research Institute for Counselling (CERIC)

The Canadian Education and Research Institute for Counselling (CERIC)
18 Spadina Road, Suite 200
Toronto, Ontario, Canada M5R 2S7
Tel: (416) 929-2510
www.ceric.ca

05 04 03 02 01 1 2 3 4 5

Library and Archives Canada Cataloguing in Publication

Van Norman, Marilyn, date
From my perspective-- : a guide to university and college
career centre management / Marilyn Van Norman.

Also available in electronic format.

ISBN 978-0-9687840-8-2

1. College placement services--Canada--Administration.
2. Counseling in higher education--Canada--Administration.
I. Canadian Education and Research Institute for Counselling
II. Title.

LB2343.5.V35 2009 378.1'9425068 C2009-901202-2

Book Design: Communicreations
www.communicreations.ca

Printed and bound in Canada. Printed on acid-free paper that is forestry friendly
(100% post-consumer recycled paper) and has been processed chlorine free.

CONTENTS

INTRODUCTION

When I started consulting for the Canadian Education and Research Institute for Counselling (CERIC), my first responsibility was to write a publication on career centre management. My initial thought was that, having been the Director of the University of Toronto Career Centre for sixteen years, this was a topic with which I was very familiar. I then considered just who a potential audience would be and what they might want to gain from reading this publication. As there are currently so many talented career centre directors and managers, all with their own approaches, I decided to simply reflect on my experience and share what I hope will be helpful tips on successful career centre management. ***From My Perspective...*** is just that—a guide to career centre management from my perspective.

Managing a career centre is both challenging and extremely fulfilling—though not without its frustrating moments, for sure. This publication has been written so that both the beginner and the more experienced director/manager will be able to take away some ideas and approaches that will prove useful in their work. Although my background is in career centre management in a university setting, I think the principles would apply to any career centre or service.

Career centre management relies on a myriad of **skills** and **competencies** including a solid understanding of career development, sound management skills, marketing, strong leadership and vision. Successful directors/managers are those who are never satisfied with the status quo. They are always looking to enhance programming, to learn all they can about the economy and the market place, to provide better services to students and employers, to find innovative ways to motivate staff and to most effectively market and promote their services. They spend time seeking their colleagues' opinions and including them in visioning exercises. They develop strategic plans based on staff and student leaders' input and establish formal and informal means by which all students and employers have the opportunity to provide feedback. Perhaps most importantly, they establish and maintain strong partnerships within the university, the profession and with key employer stakeholders.

From My Perspective... will touch upon fundamental organizational capacity issues such as staffing, financing, programming, profile establishment and maintenance, as well as essential ingredients for success such as effective networking, mentoring, relationship management, marketing, time management, visioning, strategic planning and evaluation. This publication clearly does not replace courses or seminars in any of these topics. New directors/managers might want to assess their own skill bases and seek professional development opportunities in any areas that need strengthening.

At times, managing a career centre can be a lonely endeavour. Throughout my career I found the support and friendship of directors/managers from other university and college career centres across the country to be absolutely invaluable. In that spirit I sought **input from a number of experienced colleagues from coast to coast for this publication**. Their contributions have been integrated throughout the publication. I am very grateful to all of them.

I am hopeful that you can all find something to take away from this publication that will be helpful to you within your own career centres.

LEADERSHIP

To me, strong leadership is the most important quality a successful career centre director or manager can have. Someone who commands the respect of her or his colleagues, who is able to motivate staff and who has both vision and the ability to include everyone in formulating that vision embodies the essence of leadership. **Leadership is not about being liked, but rather about being respected**. It is about team building and fostering commitment and buy-in on the part of colleagues. It is about providing strong leadership in the larger organization and direction to the department itself.

Sound leadership plays an important role in attracting and retaining good staff. A centre that can communicate its vision and mission clearly—as well as focus on the needs of students, alumni and employers—is much more likely to attract like minded staff than one that just "keeps on trucking" without any clear vision or mission. Leadership in career centre management will highlight the absolute priority of giving services to students and alumni and will focus on the importance of attracting and retaining quality employers.

Strong leaders will address issues quickly in an open, honest manner. If there are inappropriate behaviours or attitudes being observed, they will be brought to the attention of the individual(s) responsible and talked out. A plan will be devised to turn the situation around. An experienced leader will not just let the situation continue hoping it will right itself.

Good leaders will ensure that **colleagues are never put in the position of having the responsibility without the authority** for a particular program or service—nothing is more demotivating or discouraging. If an individual can be trusted with the responsibility, he or she can be trusted with the authority. Micromanaging is helpful to no one.

Leaders will also create collegial, friendly environments that offer challenging work which respects the talents and gifts everyone brings to the table. Any team needs a combination of the detail people, the big picture people, the front-line staff and the back-room number crunchers, the planners and the spontaneous folk, the presenters and the writers, the student service staff, the employer service staff and so on. A collaborative team led by someone of **vision** and **strong management** skills is what every career centre aspires to.

> Be your kind of director—don't try to adopt the style of the director who came before you or someone else. Act on what you know to be your strengths and convictions so that in the end of the day, you know that you are being true to your authentic self.
>
> — **Canadian Career Centre Director**

Career centre directors/managers can create strong teams through a number of leadership strategies in addition to those already mentioned. I always believed that it was essential to involve all staff in defining the vision and mission of the centre and annual planning, as well as five year planning. Through their contribution in determining the direction the centre is to take, staff members are in fact signing on to be major contributors to the achievement of that vision and mission for as long as they are part of the team.

Most staff want to be encouraged to grow in their positions and to know that you believe in their ability to do so. Strong leaders are always seeking ways in which staff can grow and develop their skills. In post-secondary institutions, as in many not-for-profit organizations, opportunities for promotion are often slim. To ensure that both experienced and new staff members want to stay, the leadership has to create an atmosphere that fosters personal and professional growth and development, as well as opportunities for mentoring, job shadowing and secondments. An atmosphere where satisfaction comes from working with the students, alumni and employers in a collegial, fun, team environment and where you are encouraged to continuously develop skills and experience helps to compensate for one where there are more promotions and greater pay.

It is important to demonstrate leadership outside the career centre in the rest of the university/college, in your profession, in the external community, and internationally. I will talk more about this later. Suffice it to say at this point that it enhances the credibility of your career centre for you as the director/manager to be seen as a 'mover and shaker'—a leader.

An integral part of being a strong leader is, as one of my colleagues noted, the ability to know yourself—know your strengths, but especially know your weaknesses. Work on the latter by taking courses, attending professional development sessions, and surrounding yourself with colleagues whose strengths are in the areas in which you feel weak.

Leadership is a skill that can take you a long way. It certainly helps you to build a strong team of colleagues whose focus is on the needs of students, alumni and employers. It also helps to create a 'happening career centre'—one which is respected by students, staff, faculty and employers alike.

STRUCTURE

There really is no best way to organize a career centre. In fact, all career centres are structured somewhat differently. Size, history and available resources are usually responsible for the structure of a centre. There are basically two models of career centres. One sees a focus on employment services with career counselling being offered in partnership with the counselling service at the college/university; the other which is increasingly popular is an integrated model with both employment services and career counselling being offered in the career centre.

A number of universities provide career services to individual departments or faculties. The focus of these services tends to be on marketing and employment rather than career counselling, although some universities/colleges have integrated services. Ideally, effective communication and goodwill ensures that there isn't any duplication of services, or the creation of confusion for employers. Additionally, several career centre directors are also responsible for co-op services in their colleges or universities.

Some centres are staffed by a combination of full and part-time employees. At others, students are hired to play an important role on the team. The number of staff is usually, but not always, related to the number of students and alumni served. It is always directly related to the resources allocated to the centre. In some faculties career services are more generously funded than in others.

Mandates vary according to whether employment services are the focus, whether both career counselling and employment services are offered or whether services are also available to alumni. Some centres serve alumni for one to two years after graduation while others provide services for life. Online employment listings are either available through external organizations or through a custom-built online job posting service designed for the individual college or university. In the latter case, marketing and employer relations are key functions of the centre's work.

My experience is that in a busy career centre, marketing is often overlooked in favour of staffing for direct service to students and employers. This is a mistake when offering custom-built online listings. Job listings are an essential service to students—the more diverse and plentiful, the better. As the skills required for marketing are frequently not the skills called for in advisers and counsellors, it is often necessary to extend a hiring search to include external marketing specialists. Marketing will be discussed in further detail later in the publication.

Whether one has a team centred structure or not, team building is essential to a smooth running effective service. Team building occurs through many different venues. Sharing the vision and mission into which all staff have had input is the first step to building a strong team. Excellent communications within the centre would rank a close second. Team building happens quite naturally through professional development activities, working together to produce large events, shared lunches and after work get togethers.

Teams may not work in a smaller service or make sense regardless of size. While the structure of a centre is important, it does not dictate the success of the centre. It is but one of the many considerations. What is important is to ensure that, in whatever structure exists, all staff members have a voice.

Many centres function in a traditionally hierarchical manner with a director/manager, and perhaps depending on size, an associate director, managers and/or co-ordinators of programs or services. I had the opportunity at the University of Toronto, St. George campus, to shift from a hierarchical structure with managers and co-ordinators to that of a team model. There were four main teams—career counselling and promotion, marketing and employer relations, information and career resources and information systems. Additionally there was a Career Management Consultant who worked with all of the teams and co-ordinated faculty/academic department specific workshops. At that time, as I was also Director of Student Services, an Associate Director was responsible for the day to day operation of the Centre.

What were the advantages of the teams? The first advantage was that a layer or two of hierarchy was removed, thereby allowing more direct input from all staff. This change in structure was done in part because staff often complained that their ideas and suggestions were not reaching the management team for implementation. The development of teams allowed every staff member's voice to be heard. At the same time each individual felt a direct sense of responsibility for the effective functioning of her/his team.

For each team there were facilitators who were responsible for co-ordinating the work and ensuring effective communication with the other teams. That was always a challenge as people would get so busy with their own work that cross-team communication often took a back seat. The team approach stimulated innovative programming and there was some healthy competition between teams. It appeared that being a member of a team enhanced all members' sense of responsibility as well as, of belonging.

STAFFING

The effectiveness of any centre is dependant on the quality of its staff—plain and simple! Staff members must have a sound understanding of career development, a genuine interest in the client group, a positive attitude, an appreciation of teamwork and a commitment to making the centre the best it can be. Recent years in post secondary institutions have seen an increased emphasis on accountability and outcomes—both individually and organizationally. This enhanced focus on accountability and outcomes has increased the need for working closely with individuals and providing on-going 'check-ins' with staff members.

Something that took almost my entire career to truly appreciate was that **when one is hiring or promoting, it helps to look for just two fundamental qualities—intelligence and attitude**. These, along of course with the required education and skills, will serve the organization well. The specific content of most jobs can be learned if people have the requisite academic and experiential backgrounds—intelligence cannot. Helping someone shift his/her attitude takes valuable time and energy and is not always effective.

Sami was hired to staff the front desk of a busy career centre. Problems emerged during his first week, when students complained that he had been rude to them. When asked about it, Sami's response was that they were asking stupid questions and he didn't have time to waste on stupidity. Needless to say, Sami did not last long with that attitude despite his intelligence and breadth of skills.

Tara was promoted to a position based on her seniority and commitment to the career centre. Unfortunately, enough consideration was not given to her ability to understand the complexities of the position to which she was promoted. It did not take long for her employer and in fact, Tara herself, to realize the mistake that had been made. She was simply not capable of taking on the responsibilities inherent in the position. Clearly, the job was beyond her abilities. Sadly, the promotion ended up hurting both Tara and the centre.

The qualities we all look for in career centre staff include initiative, innovation, creativity, knowledge of the economy, jobs and employment trends and a can-do attitude. It may seem like a given, but a genuine liking and respect for students is essential. One thing that all of us who work in educational settings know for sure is that if staff members are not interested in or, in fact, don't like students, they will not last very long—witness the case study earlier of Sami. During my career in post secondary institutions, I have seen more than one employee choose or be asked to leave because of their attitude towards students. They were unable or unwilling to understand our **student centred approach**. Students are the only reason any of us has a job and students must always be our top priority.

I think most career centre directors/managers would agree that staff development and management can be a very time consuming process. I found that the most time was spent with staff at the two extremes—the poor performers and the 'stars.' The latter because they demand the attention and I wanted to keep motivating and challenging them and the former because I spent an inordinate amount of time working directly with them to help them meet the challenges they faced.

Finding and hiring experienced career counsellors is a challenge. In large centres it is possible to hire individuals with a Masters Degree in Behavioural Sciences and train them in career development. That luxury is not available to smaller centres that require the career counsellor to hit the road running. One approach that has proven successful in centres across the country is that of offering an internship or practicum for students completing a M.A. in Counselling, a M.Ed. or M.S.W.. Another approach being used in some centres is that of hiring someone with an undergraduate degree who has demonstrated great potential and who wishes to complete a graduate degree. University funding would be helpful in facilitating this happening.

Hiring staff, whether continuing, part-time or students, is just step one in the process of developing an effective team. A thorough orientation period and training on the specifics of your centre and college/university are also key to ensuring that staff feel secure in the new environment and equipped to meet the challenges to come. Depending on the position for which you are hiring, there is sometimes a need for training in the actual content of the work. Time spent doing this will pay off in the future.

Professional Development often gets lost in the busy atmosphere of most career centres or relies on a few people each year attending a CACEE or CANNEX-US Conference. While these conferences are invaluable in terms of content as well as networking, in-house professional development is essential as well. Not only does it allow you to focus on particular topics you think would be of value to your colleagues, but it also provides a wonderful team building opportunity. Closing the centre twice per year for professional development is, in my opinion well worth doing. It is also possible to hold mini PD sessions at the start or end of the day, particularly if your centre is closed to students at those times.

Performance Reviews are as you all know, an opportunity to focus on an individual's contributions and goals for the upcoming year and not the punitive process they are sometimes seen as being. Although often not formally permitted in unionized environments, staff members usually welcome the opportunity to sit

Invest in their professional development, empower them, provide challenging opportunities and build a team that respects one and other. The latter can be difficult given differences that exist in terms of personal characteristics of those providing service to employers and those providing counselling, advice or consulting services to students and alumni.

— **Canadian Career Centre Director**

down and discuss their work. I always felt that individuals had the right to have the opportunity of doing this if they wished. Where there were no union rules around performance review, most staff welcomed the opportunity to give their opinion of the year, to hear a fair assessment of their work, and discuss their goals and learning plans for the coming year. In a team environment this process is determined by the team members through mutual agreement.

Job Shadowing is an interesting and, I believe, beneficial program to offer. Members of the staff are asked to volunteer to be shadowed and then those positions are advertised as available for either a half or full day of shadowing. Once it is sorted out who is shadowing whom, the individuals involved arrange between themselves when the shadowing will occur. Job Shadowing allows staff a new understanding of others' work and challenges. It also provides the opportunity for insight into the interconnectedness of each other's work. Making it work takes patience and flexibility, but the rewards outweigh the challenges.

Job Sharing is something that, when it works, is excellent for the staff involved as well as for the organization. The key in my experience is to ensure adequate time for the people sharing the job to communicate with each other. Ideally this means overlapping for a half or full day, but if that is not financially possible, the use of notes, e-mails and phone conversations becomes essential. Those on the staff doing the job sharing must be committed to making it work.

When writing about the structure I mentioned that teams allow for all staff voices to be heard. It is also obviously possible to facilitate staff participation in a more hierarchical structure when the desire to do so exists. Including all staff in visioning and the setting of future goals not only maximizes the range of ideas but also ensures buy-in and a greater commitment. At the University of Toronto before we moved to a team structure, I used to meet with groups of staff several times a year just to get their read on how things were going and what they would like to see added to the centre's programming. These meetings were in addition to all staff being included in vision and mission work.

What else helps to motivate staff besides feeling that they have an integral role in determining the direction of the centre? Staff who feel valued tend to want to give the most back. That sense of being valued might come from Professional Development opportunities, Job Shadowing, positive feedback on jobs well done, being considered for promotions, social events, office lunches or other ideas that demonstrate appreciation. In a busy centre it is too easy to neglect these forms of recognition.

Job satisfaction often depends on the nature and variety of the work. It increasingly depends on the organization's respect for balance in an employee's life. Younger staff will demand it while their older colleagues certainly appreciate it. What does balance mean? It can mean flexible hours, work from home, additional holidays, personal days, on-site affordable child care facilities and time off for elder care, to name just a few examples. In my experience, it is the exception that these benefits are abused.

In summary, **staff members make the centre**. As a result, hiring, training, motivating, providing opportunities for team building, respecting work/life balance, and inclusion in determining vision and direction are all essential components for building a successful career centre. As a director/manager you cannot invest enough in staff development, recognition or input. It sometimes might feel that you are spending an inordinate amount of time on staff issues, but it is well worth it. A happy and satisfied staff will provide the counselling, advising and employment services your students, recent graduates, alumni and employers have a right to expect. And it is the staff that will make your centre a great one.

FINANCIAL MANAGEMENT

All centres have core funding whether it comes from a student fee, the university/college, alumni, a department, faculty or a combination of these. Of course core funding is never enough! It is common to see ninety percent of a career centre budget being used for salaries and benefits, leaving little for career resources, events, promotion, marketing, new programming, much less given costs such as telephone and printing. Today, the idea of offering new services with a price tag through core funding is the exception rather than the rule.

In addition to ensuring that your centre is within budget, financial planning is an integral part of a director/manager's role. Annually analyzing whether resource allocations are correct, whether full-time positions are required, or whether part-time or contract would be more effective is a key piece of financial management. Obviously, during the year it is essential to stay on top of spending and to anticipate unforeseen expenses.

For an innovative director/manager, there are always new programs, projects or services for students or employers that could be provided. There are several possibilities for getting additional funding. Trying to get your core funding increased is the place to start. When a centre is student fee funded, my experience has been that looking to students for an increase in funding for something they understand and support is the most effective means of increasing budgets. Looking to the college/university for increased funding can be a much bigger issue as most post secondary institutions are in a constant state of financial challenge and academic priorities do take precedence for any unallocated funds.

If funding is not available through the core funding route, grants become the next place to look. A first step as most of you know, is to research where available money might be found. Possible sources include government, foundations and corporations (as long as your Development Office agrees to the latter). Once you know who a possible source of funding might be, the next step is to write a compelling proposal. Proposal writing takes time—often time you do not have. However, it is a necessary part of attaining additional monies.

> Attaining base budget funding is critical, as one time only (OTO) and soft dollar funding assist with projects but, by their nature, are not adequate sources of funding to build a stable unit which can respond effectively to needs.
>
> — **Canadian Career Centre Director**

I am sure each of you has your own funding success story. Although it took some time to develop, my philosophy is that if you don't ask you don't receive. The effort it takes to explore funding sources is, to my mind, time well spent, even though it is often time and resources you just don't feel that you have at that moment. It is imperative that you make the time.

I would like to share the story of funding of the University of Toronto's Career Centre's Extern Program. In 1987, I applied for and received an Innovation Grant from the Federal Government to start the Extern Program, which provides students with the opportunity to job shadow in a career area of their choice during Reading Week or the first week after exams in May. At the time there were just two Extern programs in existence, both in universities in the United States. That initial grant was for three years and covered all the costs of the program.

In the third year, knowing that the Innovation Program was coming to an end and that there was no chance of renewal, I wrote a proposal to The Counselling Foundation of Canada for funding for the now firmly established Extern Program. We were very fortunate to receive funding for two years. As that grant was coming to an end I went to the students through the Council of Student Services (COSS) at the University of Toronto to ask for funding to continue the program. At this point more than 2,500 students had participated during the five years and had all provided extremely positive evaluations. The students on COSS were impressed enough to vote in favour of incorporating the costs of the Extern Program into the Career Centre budget. The program is now in its 21st year thanks to a combination of government, foundation and student fees. I only wish that every initiative received such positive funding results.

A number of career centres across the country are charging employers for job listings as a way to increase funding for their centres. Further, many charge user fees for assessment tools and registration fees for job, career and professional and graduate school fairs. Career centres have to always be on the look out for innovative and lucrative ways to enhance funding.

For fifteen years the University of Toronto Career Centre was also most fortunate in partnering with the Federal Government's Human Resource Development Canada and The Counselling Foundation of Canada in the annual NATCON conference held in Ottawa. The University of Toronto Career Centre was responsible for the organization of the conference and received an administrative fee for its work from the conference funders, The Counselling Foundation of Canada. To this day, the proceeds from that fee help fund technology and program growth at the Career Centre. Personally, my role as Chair of NATCON was one of the true highlights of my career.

PROGRAMMING AND SERVICES

To some extent, programming and the services offered are dependent on the students, alumni and employers you serve, the scope of your mandate and, of course, the resources available to you. It is also dependant on the services provided directly to employers. If the centre has its own employment listing service, there will be a greater emphasis on services to employers than if it doesn't.

As you certainly all know, some of the common services offered by a career centre to students include:

- a career resource library
- a graduating students' service
- alumni services
- employment advising
- career counselling
- on-campus recruitment
- online employment listings
- summer and part-time employment services
- marketing
- employer liaison

Examples of the typical programming offered by career centres to students include:

- résumé and covering letter critiques
- job search workshops
- researching careers
- employment/volunteer listings
- interview techniques workshops
- discovering skills and options
- exploring interests and values

- networking
- self marketing
- using the Internet to look for work
- faculty specific workshops
- negotiating job offers
- workshops on completing graduate/ professional school applications
- managing one's career workshops

Many centres additionally offer job and professional/ graduate school fairs, career information events, volunteer opportunity fairs, employment etiquette sessions, skills and personality assessments, mock interviews, mentoring programs, web based workshops, specialized services for students with disabilities, international students and Aboriginal students, career conferences for students and other creative events intended to help students/alumni both develop a career goal as well as find employment.

Centres that have an integrated service of employment and career counselling usually also have fairly extensive career resources in their career resource libraries, as well as online where students are encouraged to research career possibilities. Both individual career counselling and career development workshops are offered. These may cover topics such as discovering skills and options, exploring interests and values, personality tests such as the Myers-Briggs or other interest/ personality tests, as well as networking and self marketing.

I have to admit to a bias when it comes to testing. I tend to think that tests may sometimes be a lazy approach to career counselling. I know that is heresy in some circles, but to me sitting and actually listening to a student can illicit deeper and more extensive information than any test can. The Myers-Briggs is an exception to this bias as I do think it can be invaluable to a student's self understanding and career decision making.

A number of universities/colleges offer online career development modules and courses for students. Some offer online career counselling. Online career development programs will no doubt continue to grow as technology advances. The immediacy of online services definitely appeals to students.

Some universities with a large graduate school, offer a Graduate Dossier Service which sees graduate students' CVs being sent to the universities of their choice in application for academic openings. This is a much appreciated service and provides immediate credibility for the centre in the eyes of graduate students. It is a somewhat expensive service to run as it is labour intensive, albeit less so since the advent of enhanced technology. However, it is seen by graduates of many departments as essential to their successful academic search. Increasingly there are alternatives to career centre run dossier services emerging.

There are a number of universities and colleges that have specific career development services for Aboriginal students and/or students with disabilities. Targeted programs are also offered to individual academic departments/faculties.

In universities with graduate programs it is important to offer workshops, panels, counselling and events specific to the needs of graduate students and to develop and foster strong ties with the graduate student union. Popular sessions for graduate students are CV critiques, panels on looking for non-academic work, the academic interview and networking in an academic environment.

The 21st century has brought with it an emphasis on student learning outcomes for career development services, as well as for all other student services. I have to admit that I found this 'epiphany' somewhat interesting as in my experience over the past thirty years in student services, all programming and services

Right now I am very attuned to the need to do student learning assessment. Our plan is to assess each of our student interventions to determine what students are learning (self report and objective measure where possible). I've just gotten a few faculty members on board and we're submitting a proposal for some funding. It is really important that we determine what impact we have on student learning regarding career development.

— Canadian Career Centre Director

had always been based on student learning outcomes—we had just never formalized or named the process. Despite this tinge of cynicism, I really do believe that formalizing student learning outcomes is an excellent exercise for staff and is of definite benefit to students. It forces staff to focus on what they want students to learn from each activity, workshop, counselling session, program or event and how to best assess the learning, while allowing students to understand what they are able to do and know as a result of their participation in the career activity.

As those of you who have incorporated student learning outcomes into your process already know an example of a student learning outcome from a Skills and Options workshop might be—the students will be able to identify and articulate four skills and two possible career areas where those skills might be used. Long before the introduction of student learning outcomes, counsellors would design workshops with those exact same outcomes in mind; now they have become an integrated piece of career centre programming.

In planning programming in a career centre, particularly one located in a post secondary institution, it is important to think about where the students are and what they consider to be important. Despite the fact that we would all like students to understand the importance of career development and to start using the career centre in first year, most undergraduate students, other than those in career programs, unfortunately do not start to think much about their careers until they are close to graduation.

What students do think about though are résumés. Most students work during their school years and know that they need a résumé. Promoting a résumé clinic or service to students early in the year and giving it the physical profile it deserves in the career centre draws students. We all know that résumé critiquing provides an excellent opportunity to help students identify their skills and interests. It also provides the opportunity for referrals for career counselling for students struggling with what they might like to do after graduation. Most importantly résumé services get students in the door of the career centre.

I always found input from students to be essential in determining future programming. Exploring the needs and wants of students through advisory committees, focus groups and the opinions of individual students often opened windows of opportunity not necessarily considered by me or my colleagues.

To me the establishment of a **student advisory committee** early in the year and the scheduling of four to five meetings throughout the year—always of course accompanied by food—was one of my most important responsibilities. It was essential to have a diverse group of students with representatives from the elected student groups, large faculties, LGBTQ, international and Aboriginal student groups. In addition to providing me with much enjoyed direct student contact, many valuable ideas came out of those meetings.

Students on advisory committees and in clubs and residences also provided opportunities to do joint programming with their student groups and unions. Co-sponsoring an event increased the promotion and often brought in students who had previously never attended career centre events. Students involved with the career centre become its most effective advocates.

Joint programming with academic departments can enhance relationships and also allows for more intense promotion of the event. Again topics will be of direct interest to the department doing the joint programming.

Employers are another invaluable source of student programming ideas. Their feedback often gave rise to new and innovative programming. One example of this was the implementation of the first etiquette session at University of Toronto Career Centre after hearing feedback from an employer about the table manners of some of our students at a corporate lunch which was part of the hiring process. The students loved these sessions and said that they were very helpful to them. Feedback from employers also reflected the difference the sessions made.

Employers are invaluable in participating in career centre programming whether it be by sitting on résumé and covering letter or interview panels or by attending career nights. Students think of an employer's word as being 'gospel' and so their participation is affirming of the work the centre does.

The benefit to the employer is an enhanced profile for his/her organization.

Services to employers may include the listing of employment opportunities whether they be full-time, part-time, summer or volunteer, on campus recruiting including the collection of résumés, sign-ups for interviews and the provision of interview rooms and facilitating the opportunity to meet specific groups of students whether for information sessions, briefing sessions and/or social events, as well as consulting on branding on campus and recruitment strategies.

Designing career development programs is a much bigger topic than can be addressed in this publication. Many conferences such as CANNEXUS, CCIA, CACEE, NACE, CAFCE and CACUSS offer interesting program planning sessions which are both helpful in and of themselves but also trigger your own programming thoughts.

TIME MANAGEMENT

One of the skills that has served me well over my career has been effective time management. This skill has also allowed me to manage the balance of work and life effectively. Throughout my career I have always worked hard. However, when I left for the day, the week-end or for vacation, I really left. I know that this can be a real challenge for some people. Yet, as a colleague remarked, having a life outside of work will help put the 'crazy' days into perspective, while providing the life balance we all need.

When I reflect on what it was that I did that allowed me to manage my time effectively, the first thing that comes to mind is that I realized early on in my career that I got more desk work done between 7:30 a.m. and 9:00 a.m. than I did the rest of the day. There were no phone calls, meetings or drop-ins. I could concentrate on clearing up e-mails, writing memos or designing programs. I know that many folk with young children or those who simply are not morning people cannot do this. For them it might be the 5:00 p.m. to 6:30 p.m. time slot that would work better. **Finding a block of time with the fewest possible interruptions is the first step to good time management**.

> Learning to delegate is essential to good management, as well as maintaining your own mental health.
>
> — **Canadian Career Centre Director**

It is for that reason that the Career Centre at the University of Toronto opens at 9:45 a.m. to students and closes three days a week at 4:00 p.m., while staff members start work at various times from 8:00 a.m. on and leave work anytime from 4:00 p.m. until 6:00 p.m. With these hours, staff members have administrative time without interruption. It is, of course, of most value to staff members who provide direct student or employer services.

Time management skills can be learned. Often it just takes examining your use of time to discover where you could make improvements to enhance efficiency. For some people the problem lies in procrastination. Others are disorganized or find it difficult to delegate.

The antidote to procrastination is to deal with issues, e-mails, phone calls and mail as soon as they arrive on your desk. By staying on top of all of these things, you will feel that you are controlling your own time, that things are getting done and that there are no piles to depress you. Procrastinating breeds more procrastination as the tasks begin to feel too daunting to even begin to address. When you make a decision to try to deal with e-mail as soon as it comes in, to return phone calls immediately and get paper off your desk by dealing with it as soon as you can, you begin to feel on top of your work. **Just touching a piece of paper once is not an urban myth!**

A clean desk, organized files, a time of day where you can work uninterrupted and prioritising your work go a long way to improving time management. Prioritizing is extremely important.

I remember a colleague asking me for help because he was always behind in his work. When we looked at his style of work it was clear that he had absolutely no priorities. He treated everything with the same degree of importance or non-importance. Deadlines were impossible for him as he was always struggling to just keep up and therefore more often than not missed deadlines. Once he stopped to look at why he was having a tough time, it became clear to him that he had to establish priorities and work accordingly. After looking at how he was using time, he began to prioritize and was amazed at how much more control he had over his work. Meeting deadlines became much easier for him.

It is sometimes helpful to keep a log of how you spend your time. Keep track for three to five days and then look for patterns. What is the balance between home and work? Did you work according to priorities or were you more reactive? Did the piles

just keep growing on your desk or were you able to deal with issues and file them? How long did it take you to respond to e-mails—voice mails? Did you feel rushed or overwhelmed? Did you feel that you and not the piles were in charge? How often were you late for meetings? How often were you double booked?

Delegation is an issue for some directors/managers. Effective time management is dependant on your ability to prioritize and delegate. However, people sometimes feel that they can do it better themselves, that they don't have time to explain it to someone else, or that there is no one to whom they can delegate. The reality is that you cannot do it all yourself and the career centre will suffer if you try. Furthermore, most staff members welcome new responsibilities and would be only too happy to help out.

Assuming that you have hired well and surrounded yourself with talented people, the act of delegating is, in fact, very easy. **Remember though, that when delegating, delegate the authority as well as the responsibility**. Otherwise you are tying the hands of the person to whom you have delegated.

Plan your day/week/month. A 'To Do List' is a helpful tool in both planning your work and prioritizing it. It can be either on paper or on a PDA. Writing the list forces you to think about what is most important and to become aware of any deadlines. Being able to check off a 'To Do List' is very satisfying. Try not to book back to back meetings or appointments. Give yourself a chance during the day to return voice mails and e-mails. Always take a lunch break.

Tremendous amounts of time can be wasted in setting up meetings. It is helpful to give attendees several different dates and times and a deadline to respond. Once the date is set, confirm by e-mail. If you are chairing, decide what it is you want the meeting to cover, in what order, length of time and location. Send the agenda out ahead of time if possible so that everyone attending can think about the issues before the meeting.

The topic of time management cannot be addressed without talking about a) the need for vacations and b) coverage during vacations. Too many directors feel that they are simply too busy to take holidays and just keep putting them off. This is done to the detriment of themselves, their colleagues and the organization. Everyone needs a break—a time away from work—a time to relax, enjoy a change of pace and perhaps venue—a time for renewal. In order for that renewal to take place it is essential that there be someone in place to take over during the Director's vacation. Staying in touch via e-mail or phone during vacation defeats the purpose of taking a holiday. So, when you leave on vacation—as hard as this might be—consider leaving that Blackberry in your desk!

To me, time management is essential to maintaining one's sanity. By learning how to better manage time, one will also be learning how to better manage stress. **You, not the work, will be in charge**.

NETWORKING

Networking is an integral component of a director/manager's life. No one knows the importance of excellent networking skills better than a career development professional. Few conversations with students, recent graduates or alumni take place without including the importance of networking.

Despite thoroughly understanding the essential role of networking, we often fall into the trap of thinking that we really don't have the time to do it. What do we lose by this belief? We lose the opportunity to meet people who may be helpful to our career centre, as well as to us professionally and personally. I think we all take advantage of conferences to network, but are we conscious of networking on a daily basis? Do we go out of our way to attend 'Networking Breakfasts'? Do we consciously network in our colleges and universities? Do we take advantage of employers being on campus and take time to network with them? Do we give networking the priority status it deserves?

Networking on campus includes reaching out to colleagues in other student services, faculty, academic advisors and student leaders. Meeting for coffee or lunch, seeking input and feedback, and co-sponsoring events are just some of the ways of establishing contact.

It is equally important to build strong networks with colleagues in career centres across the country and internationally. It is through the sharing of information and strategies that you as a director will grow. I know that the support and camaraderie that I enjoyed with colleagues inside as well as outside the career centre was truly valued.

For those of us who are Myers-Briggs introverts, the very thought of networking is often enough to cause whim-whams in the tummy. However, like most of our experience of living in an extroverted world, we have to dig deep, develop a strategy and just do it. The more experienced we are, the easier it becomes. I remember prior to going to my first networking event early on in my career, a colleague suggested to me that I think of a couple of current topics to raise if the conversation lagged. I keep that in mind to this day.

Networking, whether it is to increase the number of employers visiting your campus, to enhance the profile of the career centre in the college/university, or to further your own career aspirations, is an activity well worth the time spent.

The most consistent, major challenge that we deal with is resourcing. Building relationships across the campus is key in terms of developing support for budget requests, whether with student government, faculties/deans, or senior administration.

— Canadian Career Centre Director

MENTORING

Mentoring has throughout history been a powerful personal and career development tool. It has a proven track record in helping people advance in their careers. Many of us have had the privilege of being both a mentor and a 'mentee' and have experienced the richness both roles have to offer.

Mentoring is increasingly becoming an integral part of career centre offerings for students and recent graduates. Programs take the form of tri-mentoring, alumni mentoring students/new grads, faculty mentoring students interested in an academic career and older students mentoring first year students. **Everyone wins in mentoring programs**.

Many colleges/universities offer mentoring programs for staff and faculty. Whether you are officially a mentor or someone people have unofficially looked to as a mentor, I am sure that you have been helpful in providing career guidance over the years to younger or less experienced colleagues. Often a professional relationship forms without either of you identifying it as mentoring. Yet, that is exactly what it is. You may find yourself taking a particular interest in the career of one of your colleagues and going out of your way to be supportive to that person. Perhaps a colleague will seek you out for career advice or suggestions. A true mentoring relationship can be one of the most pleasant professional relationships one can have. It is one of mutual trust, respect and honesty.

While being a mentor to someone else is extremely rewarding, having a mentor yourself can be one of the highlights of your career. Your mentor's wisdom, guidance, support and ability to simply listen to you can be invaluable. Often it is the mentor's insight and understanding of the politics of the organization that is most helpful and prevents you from making career-altering miscues. The interest in you and support that you receive are frequently the confidence boosts you need at a given point of time.

One of my mentors stands out for being most helpful in the questions he would ask. His questions really made me think about what was important, why I was doing what I was doing and how I might do it differently. He was never judgemental and was always supportive. I treasure the advice and encouragement he and other mentors gave me over the years. Those relationships guided me in my own mentoring experiences.

> Find one or two mentors who can help guide your career and give you sound advice.
>
> — **Canadian Career Centre Director**

While the next chapter will deal with establishing your profile on and off campus, networking and mentoring are the foundational pieces necessary for profile enhancement. The larger your network, the more opportunity you have for spreading the word about the career centre, its programs and services. Your mentors will help you spread the word about the centre and the excellent work it does.

ESTABLISHING YOUR PROFILE

A reality in all post secondary institutions is that faculty members and academic departments/faculties are the college's/university's top priorities and have the highest profiles in the institution. And...so they should. Student services such as career centres have to work at establishing and maintaining their profiles within the college or university—firstly with students and secondly with faculty, staff and senior administrators. Profile development may be one of the more important things a centre can do. It is certainly a huge factor in funding. To my mind it has to be one of the director/manager's top priorities.

How does a career centre ensure a high profile in a university or college with faculty, staff and senior administrators? My experience has been that the better known the director was the higher profile the career centre enjoyed.

I was fortunate to have had an example set by my predecessor who sat on a multitude of university committees, had a major role in organizing U of T Day and chaired the university's United Way campaign. I could clearly see that the very high profile she established on campus was of direct benefit to our career centre.

In following her wise example when I became Director I worked my way onto many university-wide committees and college councils. I was Acting Status of Women officer on a part-time basis for the university for a period and chaired several campus committees. These were just a few of the ways in which I tried to do my part to raise the Career Centre's profile in the university. Certainly, by participating in the university or college in this way you do get the attention of the senior administration and by association they gain awareness of the Career Centre and its function. It is equally important to facilitate staff becoming involved in university/college committees. The key to being able to participate on committees outside the centre is excellent time management skills and the ability to prioritize.

Maintaining a high profile with the general student or alumni body is probably most effectively done via word of mouth. If students and alumni are having good experiences at the career centre, they will tell their friends and encourage them to also go to the centre. Survey after survey shows that next to the web, friends are the most common referral.

It is essential to put adequate resources into the design and maintenance of the career centre website. The web is students' prime resource for all things important and has to be kept up-to-date to maintain credibility. This is equally true for the employer website.

Large, well-attended events such as career days, job fairs, and special events draw students' attention as well. For many these may be their first exposure to the career centre. Students will wander over to see why the crowd is there and what they may be missing.

I felt strongly that each year it was essential for me to establish a positive rapport with all student leaders. I would contact them immediately after hearing the results of an election to congratulate them and to invite them to lunch. I would follow up with partnering ideas, which were normally welcomed, and with several subsequent lunches during the year. My efforts always paid off. Firstly, I had the privilege of getting to know some of the brightest, most creative students at the university; even more importantly, the student leaders knew that they were partners with the Career Centre in offering programming to students. The strength of these relationships always paid off both at budget time and in programming ideas.

To gain the interest of academic departments it was always important to seek out the individual faculty members who were more likely to have an interest in students' lives after graduation. This was easy to do in departments or faculties such as commerce, engineering and computer science, but it was often more of a challenge with humanities and science departments. For example, I remember one zoology professor who, in responding to my question as to where zoology undergrads went after graduation said "Why would I care what they do if they are not pursuing an academic career?" He was perfectly serious. Fortunately, there was usually at least one faculty member students identified as interested in their futures, even if those futures did not involve academic careers. After identifying individuals who might be have been helpful, it was useful to put them on lists to receive promotional materials, invite them to Open Houses and to ask if class announcements could be made during their classes.

In my experience, holding Open Houses was an effective way to engage staff from the registrar's office, librarians, student advisers, chairs, financial aid staff and other university/college staff and faculty. It seemed that holding the Open House at the beginning of the day and supplying a breakfast elicited the largest turnouts.

Try to gain a clear understanding of the goals and direction of your institution. Think strategically not only about how the career centre fits with the institution's goals, but also about what are the possibilities. Then make sure that you communicate to faculty and administrators what the Career Centre does and how it supports the institution's mission.

— **Canadian Career Centre Director**

Being known in the college or university is paramount to offering effective services. You could have the most extensive array of services and programs but if students don't know about them, they aren't much use. And, if you do not enjoy the support of faculty and senior administrators, on-going funding could be in jeopardy. As I said earlier, **raising the profile of the career centre has to be one of the director/manager's top priorities** and is built on the foundation of skillful networking and often, mentoring.

MARKETING TO EMPLOYERS

Marketing to potential employers of college and university students and graduates is a challenge faced by all schools with their own job listing services. To ensure credibility and to maximize opportunities for students and graduates, marketing has to be given serious consideration. As I mentioned earlier all too often in our environments, usually due to financial constraints, we add marketing to a staff member's already busy job. This creates two problems—one, the staff member does not have the skills or experience required to be effective in marketing and two, as a result, that individual concentrates on the more comfortable parts of the job. Thus, marketing takes a back seat.

What I learned the hard way over the years was **to 'find' the money to hire an experienced marketing specialist** who understood the public sector and, ideally, the employment market for new graduates. If you are fortunate enough to be able to hire an experienced marketing expert, he or she will come with an established network, strategies for developing and maintaining relationships with current employers and for reaching out to potential employers. If the marketers have had experience in the public sector they will have a myriad of methods of marketing without incurring large costs. They will know how to effectively use an employer website to draw employers to your centre as well as the strategic use of targeted Internet, e-mail and brochure campaigns.

Your employer website is extremely important and warrants both the time and money necessary to build and maintain a professional looking and easily accessed site. Getting input from employers about website key ingredients is always useful.

Where do the career centre practitioners fit into a marketing strategy? You and your career centre colleagues know the student body and alumni at your college or university better than anyone else. You are able to articulate to a marketer about what makes your students and graduates unique, how their education allows them to be the best prepared for the world of work and what their value is to an employer. From hearing students talk about their career interests, you also know which sectors should be recommended for the marketer's attention. However, perhaps most importantly, all staff members have their own networks which no doubt include potential new employers. Promoting the college/university's students and graduates to potential employers ought to be part of every staff member's job description and something to which everyone is committed.

In the students you have the product. If yours is like many career centres you will have varied your approach of how to define the 'product' and how to pitch it. In my time at the University of Toronto we varied between marketing the students—their brightness, diversity, talent, breadth of disciplines, to marketing the University—largest in Canada, downtown Toronto, diverse student body, range of faculties and programs, illustrious alumni, Nobel prize winning professors and so on. We finally concluded that the reality was that the 'products' really were the students and alumni—not the university.

In employers of students, recent graduates and in some cases alumni, you have the market. It is essential to build strong networks with current employers while at the same time attracting new ones. Although students are the top priority, employers rank a very close second. Establishing and maintaining strong relationships with employers is essential to their continuing to recruit on campus. The availability of efficient interview facilities, processes in place that ensure the appropriate student is present and well prepared to be interviewed, the provision of lunch or suggestions of nearby restaurants, a comfortable employer lounge and friendly, helpful staff members all contribute to encouraging employers to keep coming back to the college/university.

In part, the marketing strategy defines what sets the 'product' apart from the competition—students, recent graduates and alumni from other colleges and universities. It focuses on what makes them unique and of value to an employer. It is sometimes helpful to do the S.W.O.T. analysis to help define what the strengths of your campaign are, what the weaknesses are, where the opportunities lie and to identify any threats to the campaign.

Equally important is determining the targets of your marketing plan—for example, specific areas such as advertising, publishing, laboratories, as well as potential employers of a particular faculty such as engineering or pharmacy. Decisions will also be made on whether to target multinationals, large, medium, small organizations and private or public sector employers. Research and input from career centre staff and students will help establish target areas.

Decisions have to be made in terms of approach—networking events, company visits, direct mail campaigns, e-mail, billboards, radio, TV, Internet. In my experience, although often the popular choice of staff, I found that company visits were the least effective use of time in marketing. A half or even a full day may be spent with one company during a visit, while hundreds of e-mails could be sent in the same amount of time with enhanced results. That is not to say that it is never appropriate to do company visits but, as a rule of thumb, I believe there are more effective uses of time. I do think attendance at trade shows is often very fruitful from a marketing perspective.

As entire books are written on developing marketing strategies, I have obviously just scratched the surface of planning a marketing strategy for a career centre aimed at potential employers. That professional marketer you have hired will take it from here.

PROMOTION TO STUDENTS

Promoting the career centre to students and alumni is as important as marketing to employers—in fact, more so. The old saying 'build it and they will come' is not always true for career centres. Students have to understand what's in it for them before they will take time out of their hectic days to visit the career centre or its website.

In addition to the techniques for building the profile of the centre, there are endless strategies for promoting it. These include, but are not limited to, using online resources such as your own website, hosting career related programs on student run radio stations, placing ads and career supplements in student newspapers and promoting the career centre on billboards, banners and those old traditional and, I would say, tired flyers and brochures. I should clarify, I believe that brochures are useful once the student has come into the centre to help them understand the extent of services and programs available to them, but not as a vehicle to attract them in the first place.

Today's students, as we all know, rely solely on the Internet for their information, and that is where we have to be to grab their attention. The bulk of career centre promotion these days happens online. Having an attractive, yet informative, website that is constantly updated is essential. The use of Facebook, iPods and text messaging in promoting career centres is still in its infancy, but I believe that it is well worth the time spent exploring ways to maximize their use. Students would be the best source for tips on how to make these resources work at your college or university.

In addition to the Internet, as I have noted elsewhere, having friends share their positive experiences with the career centre is a very effective promotional tool. Holding a "Tell a Friend" event can be productive. Taking advantage of high profile events such as career days or job fairs is an effective way to introduce students to the career centre. Often students would simply stumble upon an event and wonder what it was. Having staff available to fill them in and encourage them to check out the centre out for themselves is useful.

Sidewalk sign boards strategically used throughout the year can be effective in promoting both the career centre and specific events. It is important to use them sparingly. Otherwise, they may just meld into the landscape.

As I have mentioned earlier, partnering with student groups and academic departments or faculties expands the exposure that the career centre receives. Organizing joint events produces enhanced promotion, and of course there are contests. I was always of two minds when it came to using contests to attract students to the career centre. However, I do have to admit that, in fact, they are effective—but only when the prizes are felt to be really worthwhile by students.

Promoting career centre services to students, recent graduates and alumni is an extremely important component of the work of the career centre. The more students and alumni are aware of the services of the centre and the more they take advantage of them, the more successful the centre will be.

ORGANIZATIONAL PERFORMANCE

Increasingly, the results of an organizational capacity evaluation are seen as integral to running a successful career centre and feed directly into strategic planning. The assessment measures the organization's ability to meet its goals and achieve its mission. The results of effective assessments can be used to help position the career centre.

Every five years at the University of Toronto, I initiated a thorough review of the centre—its vision, mission and approach. The result of each review was a five year plan. All staff members were involved in the process, as were students on the Career Centre Advisory Committee. We would also hold focus groups of student users and employers. The staff divided into groups to study various aspects of the centre—where we were, where we would like to be and how to get there.

Sometimes the vision statement was changed. In one notable review, we designed the Self Managed Career Development Model which continues to guide programming and services at the University of Toronto Career Centre to this day. The Self Managed Career Development Model was one way of looking at the career development process. It divided the process into four fundamental parts:

- Discover Your Skills and Options
- Identify Work Opportunities
- Market Yourself for Today's Workplace
- Manage Worklife

There was no definitive starting place, but rather the model provided the opportunity for an individual to plug in wherever they thought they were on the continuum. We believed that it was as relevant for a teenager as it was for a seasoned professional considering a career change. Essential to the Self Managed Career Development Model, in addition to it being self directed, was that it stressed the importance of continuously assessing the marketplace and the impact of changes taking place.

Some of the areas traditionally included as a part of an assessment or review include strengths and weaknesses, vision and mission, organizational structure, staffing, teamwork, values, training, programming and communication.

Organizational capacity evaluations are often conducted by external consultants. Their process may include interviews with individual staff, focus groups with students and employers and feedback from internal partners such as registrars and academic advisers. They often start the process by having the career centre staff gather a significant amount of information including annual reports, assessment tools, program information, budget information and organizational charts. While time consuming and expensive, some academic cultures give external reviews more credence than internal ones.

Theories and practices around student feedback to career centres have changed significantly over the years. When I first started working at the University of Toronto Career Centre, the only assessments that were done were student evaluations at the end of all workshops. From that point, satisfaction surveys were added following career/job/volunteer fairs, career information days, individual counselling sessions, Extern Program participation and the on-campus recruitment program. Students and employers completed the latter. In other words, every event/encounter was evaluated in terms of student/employer satisfaction. In addition, needs assessments were carried out annually.

When I left as Director of the Career Centre at the University of Toronto, students completed an on-line satisfaction survey of all services and programs as part of their annual registration process. As a result of it being part of their re-registration process, responses from over 25,000 students were attained each year. In analyzing this data we were able to ascertain the degree/program/gender/college/major/year in school and so on, thereby knowing to whom to promote various services and programmes. That information was invaluable to program planning.

Satisfaction surveys, although important, do not address all assessment needs. It is often too tempting to use the same satisfaction surveys for all workshops rather than design individual ones which will provide a greater depth of information. Graduate surveys are another measure of the success of the career centre's programs and services. With the advent of writing learning outcomes, all programming will be assessed according to the successful attainment of the learning outcomes.

Employer surveys help to ascertain the level of satisfaction employers enjoy when recruiting at your campus. Their feedback can also be used to lobby for things like new or enhanced interview rooms, changes to curriculum in career directed programs and improvements to the service they receive while on your campus.

Just as self assessment is integral to the career planning process, career centre evaluations are essential to ensuring that a relevant and high quality service is offered to students, alumni and employers.

STRATEGIC PLANNING

Organizations that do not take the time to define their purpose, assess where they are, where they want to be and how to best get there, may find themselves spinning their wheels and being out of touch with their clients. **Strategic Planning provides a structure for defining and meeting organizational goals**.

Fundamental questions to be asked include:

- What do we do?
- For whom do we do it?
- Why do we do it?
- What do we do best?
- What could we improve on?
- What could we be doing that we aren't doing?
- What do we want to be doing in a year, 2 years, 5 years?
- What is the ideal, what is the current reality and what will it take to achieve that ideal?

It is important to involve staff, student leaders, alumni, as well as employers in strategic planning. Not only does it provide everyone with an opportunity to stop and really look at what you are doing, how well you are doing it and what else you might be doing, it also forces the group to set priorities, goals and objectives. It allows for creative visioning without constraints and develops a sense of ownership. Most importantly, strategic planning allows the centre to develop a plan, a strategy for achieving that plan and a method of communicating the plan to the centre's users.

If the centre currently does not have a vision and mission statement, writing one will be part of the Strategic Planning process. If it does have them, the planning will provide an opportunity to revisit those statements and ensure that they are still valid. As you all know, a vision declares where an organization would like to be in the future, while a mission defines the current purpose of the organization—why they exist. Both should be short and to the point.

Developing a five year plan gives structure to the direction of the centre and helps everyone understand what the goals are and how they will be achieved. It helps students, employers and the university/college appreciate the direction of the centre. Most certainly it is essential for financial planning. An annual planning exercise is necessary to stay on top of the five year plan.

Strategic planning can be done in-house or with the help of a consultant. Hiring a well respected consultant is frequently money well spent as she/he will ensure a positive process. Often the process itself is as important as the plan that evolves from it. I would suggest that, if your centre has never done any strategic planning, a consultant to guide you through the process is well worth it.

Many of you may feel that neither you nor the centre has time to do strategic planning. You are too busy providing direct service to students, alumni and employers. While this is no doubt true, it is important to step back and look at the big picture and integrate strategic planning into your centre's priorities.

Some people believe that after doing all the work involved in strategic planning, the plan will just gather dust on some shelf. Clearly, it is the role of the director/manager to ensure that is not the case. Breaking the plan down into action plans helps to maximize the chances of implementation. It is also helpful to name one or more member of the strategic planning team to take on the responsibility of ensuring that the plan gets carried out.

CHANGE MANAGEMENT

As we all know, the only constant in our world is change. This is particularly true in the world of career centre management.

Stewarding change in any organization is an integral part of management. In an academic environment, guaranteed change occurs annually with the introduction each spring of new student leaders, principals, deans and chairs. New relationships have to be forged and the educating of our academic colleagues and student leaders on what exactly career development is needs to be begun again. Budget time is another period of change where positions may shift, downsizing may take place or, if we are really fortunate, new positions may be created.

To manage change effectively, there needs to be a clear understanding of the reasons for change, a buy-in on the part of all staff and the necessary resources, whether staff or financial. Problems managing change occur when staff members' needs are not considered, when the fact that people react differently to change is ignored, when open communication isn't present and when the abilities of staff members are underestimated. Clearly, staff members are key to effectively managing change in any environment.

Change is synonymous with the employment market. Those of us who have been around career centres for awhile have been through many economic up and down turns. We've witnessed 'student markets' and 'employer markets'. We've seen our interview rooms crammed month after month, and we have also seen them quite empty. We've seen an abundance of listings and a dearth.

As the director/manager, you are responsible for managing this change by putting resources where they are most needed according to the market. In tight markets, you need to supplement your direct services to students in order to maximize their chances of finding work in a difficult employment market, while also boosting marketing resources. In good times, additional resources are often needed in employment services to handle the demand for on-campus interviewing and the increase in listings.

If the change is going to affect staffing resources, the sooner you address the situation and talk openly about it with staff, the less misinformation will exist. Be honest, yet try to help them see the opportunities change brings. Be available to answer questions individuals may have and to hear staff feedback.

Change can be viewed as an opportunity or a threat. You aren't much help to anyone if you choose to see change as a threat. Leaders see the changes and welcome the opportunity those changes bring. Despite perhaps sounding 'Polyanna-ish', it is the truth.

CONCLUSION

Writing this publication has been an extremely interesting exercise for me. It has allowed me to reflect on the time I spent in career centre management and to recall how tremendously rewarding it was. I had the privilege of working with a very fine group of Career Centre colleagues, a high quality of students, alumni, staff and faculty at the University of Toronto, as well as wonderful employers and colleagues from other universities and colleges in Canada and around the world.

I hope to synthesize in this conclusion some of the more important lessons I learned during my tenure as a director of a university career centre. One thing that clearly stands out for me was that **I could never go wrong, if I made decisions based on what was in the best interest of students**. Asking this question whenever I was in doubt about a decision usually helped me zero in on the correct direction to take.

I believe that we are so fortunate to work in the field of career development. It is a field that touches a myriad of disciplines including economics, sociology, psychology, history, political science, marketing, international relations and education, to name just a few. It is a field in which change is constant. As a result, there is always something to learn. I am grateful to the career development profession for the understanding I garnered about the economy, its effect on the labour market and career availability.

Perhaps one of the more interesting things I learned was that career development is more often as dependant on **being in the right place, at the right time, with the right skills**, as it is on traditional methods of career planning. I know that is heresy to think, much less say in some places. However, John Krumboltz and those who believe in his theory of 'Happenstance' would certainly agree. Consider your own career path—ask your friends. How many of you or them ended up where you are because of traditional career planning techniques and how many were just in the right place, at the right time, with the right skills. I know that my personal experience has been right place, right time and right skills.

And, if I am correct that this is increasingly the case, the ability to identify skills and relate them to the world of work becomes that much more important. It never failed to amaze me how difficult university students found it to be able to articulate what their skills were, much less where they might want to use them. Even mature graduate students struggled to identify their skills. It seems to me that it would be helpful if children were taught in elementary and high school how to identify their skills as they were developing. It would certainly make skills identification for career development purposes and thinking about work options that much easier in college/university.

A management lesson I learned early on was that **loyalty, along with being fair and equitable in promoting people, is not always in everyone's best interest**. Not everyone is cut out for management, and it certainly is not doing someone a favour to put her or him in a position she or he cannot handle. That was a tough lesson for me because my intention in promoting a colleague was to be fair, yet it turned out to be a very unfair decision for all concerned. I did learn from it, albeit the hard way.

Another tough management lesson—I remember my boss telling me as I was accepting my first management position that **it was not wise to be friends with the people you supervise**. I thought at the time—what ridiculous advice. Oh, how I have learned to respect that wise piece of advice and share it with colleagues over the years. It is fine if the staff member who is also a friend always performs well and you are never in the position to have to eliminate her or his position due to financial cutbacks. If this is not the case, you are in trouble. I have seen too many situations of managers finding themselves in of the unenviable position of having to either discipline or lay off a friend.

One of my management principles was—**no surprises**. I would let colleagues who reported to me know right from the start that my least favourite thing was to be caught by surprise. What did I mean? I meant that I didn't want, for instance, to hear about something relevant to the Career Centre from someone outside the centre before being told directly. It sounds simple enough, but when one is caught flat-footed it is not only personally embarrassing but reflects poorly on the Career Centre.

I have previously mentioned my epiphany regarding hiring—**hire intelligence and attitude**; the rest can be learned. I'm not sure why it took so long for me to come to that conclusion, but it did. However, once I had it, I did some of my very best hires.

What else did I learn during my years as Director of the University of Toronto Career Centre that might be worth passing on? Certainly, one thing would be that a key relationship a director/manager has **to establish and nurture is a dynamic and positive relationship with one's boss**. It is essential to being able to develop and run an effective career centre. This relationship may have to begin with your teaching her/him a crash course on career development and where career education fits in the bigger academic picture. Your boss has to understand well enough to be able to articulate the role the career centre plays in contributing to the university's achievement of its mission. A well versed boss will then be ideally able to act as a cheerleader for the centre. Further, her or his clear understanding will serve you well at budget time.

I previously talked about the importance of profile and the role the director/manager plays in **establishing and maintaining a high profile in the university or college**. I cannot stress this enough. The higher the profile of the director/manager, the higher the profile of the career centre. A bi-product of establishing a positive profile on campus will be that you will be noticed by senior administrators and more likely to be approached to sit on university committees. The experience you gain and contacts you meet while on committees are invaluable to both you personally and to the career centre.

I believe that it is also important for directors/managers to **get involved in professional associations by accepting leadership positions**. In Canada, the associations that career centres tend to belong to are CACEE, CAFCE and CCIA. I will always treasure my experiences on the CACEE Board, both as a member and then as President. My fellow Board members were impressive representatives from employer members and colleges/universities. We did some excellent work and the association grew during our tenure, but we also really had fun. I value many of the friendships I made then to this day.

It is important to take leadership roles in professional associations, but it is equally important to **stay on top of all career related sites and services**. For example CERIC is an institute dedicated to career counselling whose committees on learning and professional development and research provide support for innovative ideas and projects. Additionally, CERIC organizes CANNEXUS, an excellent annual national career development conference. Other CERIC programs include Contact Point which is an internationally recognized and National award winning on-line resource for career development practitioners and last, but far from least, the Canadian Journal of Career Development.

In summary, in writing this publication, I have had the privilege of looking back on the part of my career that was in career centre management. I have many fine memories of that time and all I learned at the University of Toronto, CACEE and NATCON. I am so fortunate to now be able to create new career memories through my current work as National Co-ordinator, Outreach and Innovation with CERIC.